Building the
Kingdom

Daily Words of Inspiration

by
Reverend Quincy Patterson

Copyright ©2021 Reverend Quincy Patterson

All rights reserved. No part of this publication may be reproduced, distributed, or transmitted in any form or by any means, including photocopying, recording, or other electronic or mechanical methods, without the prior written permission of the publisher, except in the case of brief quotations embodied in critical reviews and certain other noncommercial uses permitted by copyright law.

Unless otherwise indicated, all Scripture quotations are taken from the Holy Bible, **New Living Translation**, copyright © 1996, 2004, 2007 by Tyndale House Foundation. Used by permission of Tyndale House Publishers, Inc., Carol Stream, IL 60188. All rights reserved.

ISBN-978-1-951300-06-7

Liberation's Publishing – West Point - Mississippi

Building the
Kingdom

Daily Words of Inspiration

Building the Kingdom

Foreword

Once we've accepted Christ as our personal Lord and Savior, knowing we're no longer living in sin is refreshing; to say the least. For many of us, when accepting Christ, it's a Godsend. Why? Because for some, it's a second chance that God's given us to get it right. As we walk with Christ, encouragement along the way is vital as we strive to find our footing. We get the needed spiritual nourishment from studying God's word (the Bible); from assembling ourselves with likeminded followers of Christ and daily devotional readings that inspire us to stay the course as we follow Christ Jesus.

"Building the Kingdom" by my great friend of almost 40 years, the Rev. Quincy Patterson; is a glorified collection of daily devotionals penned by Him that will surely make getting up in the morning worthy of giving God praise and all the glory. This collection of inspired writings will comfort you when you're feeling lost or experiencing loss, empower you when feeling tired and downtrodden and will mend any broken heart you might have. For this past half decade, he's not only talked the talk, but Rev. Patterson has walked the walk, while writing about it as well.

It is my infinite hope that you'll find this meditative collection of daily devotionals as awe inspiring and useful as l have. In the end, l feel you will be justly rewarded for your faithfulness to God, through the written words of this truly blessed servant of God. May God bless you all, now and always is my prayer.

John Martin Branson III
West Memphis AR

DAY 1

As Christians, if we are going to trust in God alone then we must continue to grow in faith. You see, faith is like a muscle. The more it's stretched the stronger it gets. When our faith is tested and tried it continues to grow and we begin to trust God more and more. Many people who call themselves Christians say that they have faith, but when the test comes, they don't exhibit faith. So then how do we get this faith? Paul says in Roman 10:17 So then faith cometh by hearing, and hearing by the Word of God. So, if we want to increase in our faith then we must increase in our intake of the Word of God.
Your day is already blessed!

DAY 2

As Christians, if we are going to trust in God alone then we must trust that we will live eternally with Christ Jesus. Not only us but all who have died in Christ. I know many of us have lost loved ones in the midst of this pandemic. We may not have been able to give them a proper homegoing celebration, but the Good News is that we will be able to see them again. When Lazarus died Jesus came to Bethany and spoke the following words to Martha, who was mourning her brother's death. "I am the resurrection and the life. Anyone who believes in Me will live, even after dying. Everyone who lives in Me and believes in Me will never ever die." John 11:25-26(NLT) Do you believe this?

Your day is already blessed!

DAY 3

As Christians if we are going to trust in God alone then we must remember that whatever we are experiencing right now is temporary. If you're facing hard trials remember they're temporary. If you're going through suffering and pain, remember it's temporary. Even if things are great and you're receiving the praises of others remember it's temporary. Even our own lives are temporary. 1 Peter 1:24-25(NLT) the scriptures says, *people are like grass; their beauty is like a flower in the field. The grass withers and the flower fades.* But the Word of the Lord remains forever. And that Word is the Good News that was preached to you. So, remember only the Word of God will endure until the end. Have A Blessed Day.

Your day is already blessed!

DAY 4

As Christians if we are going to trust in God alone then we must go to God and talk to Him no matter what is going on in our lives. James 5:13(NLT) says *Are any of you suffering hardships? You should pray. Are any of you happy? You should sing praises.* You see no matter how low we get from suffering hardships we can't forget that God is the one who can deliver us from them all. Oftentimes we allow the suffering to cause us to forget God. We tell everybody else about it but God. Then when great things happen in our lives, we should sing praises unto God. We're so busy celebrating that we forget to tell God, "Thank You." But no matter which extreme be it suffering or joy or anything in between talk to God about it.

Your day is already blessed!

DAY 5

Christians if we are going to trust in God alone then we must realize that we are called to reconcile others to Christ by sharing the gospel. Understand that every time you share the gospel with someone they are not going to always instantly come running to Christ and be changed forever. Sometimes you sharing the gospel is just the seed of someone being saved then someone else comes along and waters that seed. Eventually it's God who gives the increase. Too many people who call themselves Christians get mad when people don't respond to them sharing the gospel or when they respond to someone else sharing the gospel. We should feel that as long as the person becomes a part of the Kingdom of God who cares who they responded to. God gets the glory. So, plant a seed today and watch God give the increase.

Your day is already blessed!

DAY 6

As Christians if we are going to trust in God alone then we must realize that we must know the truth. So many people who call themselves Christians are still in bondage to the world because they keep believing the lies of the world and Satan. They base their whole lives on what the world says on social media, in the news or the people around them. This has people all confused and their moral values have been diluted. Jesus says in John 8:32 *And ye shall know the truth, and the truth shall make you free.* He didn't say that knowing about the truth, as many do know the truth. He said ye shall know the truth. Know "hear" means to be intimate with. We know that Jesus is the truth and if we are intimate with Christ Jesus then He will set us free. Do you know the truth?

Your day is already blessed!

DAY 7

As Christians if we are going to trust in God alone then we must continue to grow in the knowledge of God's Word. We can't be the Christian God wants us to be if we don't spend time with Him in His Word. Studying the Word of God is a vital part of the Christian life. We know that the Bible is God's Word because 2 Timothy 3:16-17 says *All scripture is given by inspiration of God, and is profitable for doctrine, for reproof, for correction, for instruction in righteousness: That the man of God may be perfect, thoroughly furnished unto all good works.* Doctrine tells us what's right. Reproof tells us what's not right. Correction tells us how to get right. Instructions in righteousness tells us how to stay right.

Your day is already blessed!

DAY 8

As Christians if we are going to trust in God alone then we must continue to grow in faith. Faith is our confident hope and assurance of the things that we hope for but do not see yet. Faith says we have it even before we hold it. Faith gives us the assurance that God's Word is done in the spiritual before it manifests in the natural. Hebrews 11:1 says *Now faith is the substance of things hoped for, the evidence of things not seen.* It takes faith to trust God when you don't understand what you're seeing, and it takes faith to please God. We must believe that He is and that He is a rewarder of them that diligently seek Him. Do you have now faith?

Your day is already blessed!

DAY 9

As Christians if we are going to trust in God alone then we must realize that we are commissioned by Christ to go and teach others about Him and baptize them in the name of the Father and the Son and the Holy Ghost and then teach them to observe all things that He has taught us. And He has assured us that He will be with us always even until the end of the world. Many churches today have problems with this commission because it begins with Go. We are waiting for the world to come to church instead of taking the gospel to the world. If we are fishers of men, then we have to go fishing. Even the greatest fisherman can't stand on his porch and call the fish to him he must go fishing. Many churches also fail in the 2nd teaching process. They fail teach people how to be a Christian after they become a Christian. So, we must Go Teach Baptize and Teach.

Your day is already blessed!

DAY 10

As Christians if we are going to trust in God alone then we must trust that no matter what we are facing God will supply what we need. Whether we need financial assistance or healing in our bodies or peace in our minds Philippians 4:19 says but my God shall supply all your need according to His riches in glory through Christ Jesus. So, Jesus is the answer to every need in our lives. Because He is Jehovah Jireh our provider, Jehovah Rapha our healer and Jehovah Shalom our prince of peace. So, trust that whatever you need my God shall supply.

Your day is already blessed!

DAY 11

As Christians if we are going to trust in God alone then we must understand that we can pour out our souls to God and that He will grant us our petitions. Oftentimes we are so congested with the things of this world and the worries of life that our souls get congested and causes our souls to become weary. We have to learn to do what Hannah did in 1 Samuel 1:15 &17 And Hannah answered and said No, my lord, I am a woman of a sorrowful spirit: I have drunk neither wine nor strong drink but have poured out my soul before the Lord. Then Eli answered and said, go in peace: and the God of Israel grant thee the petition that thou hast asked of Him. He will do the same for you.

Your day is already blessed!

DAY 12

As Christians if we are going to trust in God alone then we must understand that not only will God keep our souls, but He also promises to give rest to our souls. It's one thing when the body gets tired and weary, and you feel like you can't move. It's different when your soul gets weary. When our souls get weary, we don't even want to think about anything because our minds are a part of our souls and we can't even love on people as a matter of fact the ones we love most get on our nerves because the heart is a part of our souls. Jesus says in Matthew 11:28-29 Come unto Me, all ye that labour and are heavy laden, and I will give you rest. Take My yoke upon you and learn of Me; for I am meek and lowly in heart: and ye shall find rest unto your souls. So, whatever has your soul weary give it to Jesus and He will give your soul rest.

Your day is already blessed!

DAY 13

As Christians if we are going to trust in God alone then we must know that the Lord is our keeper, and He preserves our souls. It seems as if so, many things today are out to destroy us. Satan uses all types of tactics and schemes to try to overcome us. In his own subtle way Satan tries to draw us away from God because his mission is to steal and kill and destroy. But I'm so glad that the Lord is our keeper. Psalms 121:5-8 says The Lord is thy keeper: The Lord is thy shade upon thy right hand. The sun shall not smite thee by day, nor the moon by night. The Lord shall preserve thee from all evil: He shall preserve thy soul. The Lord shall preserve thy going out and thy coming in from this time forth, and even for ever more. So, don't worry God is keeping you.

Your day is already blessed!

DAY 14

As Christians if we are going to trust in God alone then we must realize that we have to depend upon God for the strength to be able to do God's will. Many people take Philippians 4:13 I can do all things through Christ who strengthens me out of context. Paul was telling the church that he could survive with a little or he could have overflow and survive but he could only do this through Christ who gives him strength. Whatever God has willed for us to do then we can do that through Christ who gives us strength. If we are trying to do something that is not in God's will then Christ does not give us the strength for that. Satan might give us that strength, but it won't come from Christ. If you need the strength to love unconditionally you can do that through Christ who strengthens you. If you need strength to forgive someone who hurt, you really bad you can get that through Christ. If you need the strength to remain humble after a big promotion you can do that through Christ. Remember whatever we need to do that's in God's will, we can do it through Christ.

Your day is already blessed!

DAY 15

As Christians if we are going to trust in God alone then we must not let fear be a hindrance in our lives. Oftentimes fear comes from a dark place in our lives or from a place of weakness. We find ourselves sometimes feeling like life is dragging us back to that dark place and we allow fear to keep us from moving forward. What we must realize is that a dark place is not so bad when you have a faithful light to show you the way. Well Psalms 27:1 says The Lord is my Light and salvation; whom shall, I fear? The Lord is the strength of my life; of whom shall I be afraid. The Lord is our Light in darkness and our strength in weakness, so we have no need to fear.

Your day is already blessed!

DAY 16

As Christians if we are going to trust in God alone then we must act as children of the Most High God. Matthew 5:9 says Blessed are the peacemakers for they shall be called the children of God. Children of God are peacemakers not peacebreakers. Too many people who call themselves Christians are hell raising peace breakers who only love themselves. Luke 6:35 says but love your enemies, and do good, and lend, hoping for nothing again; and your reward shall be great, and ye shall be the children of the Highest: for He is kind unto the unthankful and to the evil. Are you a child of the Most High?

Your day is already blessed!

DAY 17

As Christians if we are going to trust in God alone then we must be open to receive wisdom and knowledge from God. Some people who call themselves Christians think they know everything. They even think that they know what's better for them than God does. They think that way because they have no true reverence for God. True reverence is to be in awe of the greatness of God and His awesome power. But those who have no reverence for God are not open to receive wisdom and knowledge for Proverbs 1:7 says the fear of the Lord is the beginning of knowledge: but fools despise wisdom and instructions. Proverbs 9:10 says the fear of the Lord is the beginning of wisdom: and the knowledge of the Holy is understanding. So, we must have a reverential fear of the Lord to receive wisdom and knowledge, or we could just be fools.

Your day is already blessed!

DAY 18

As Christians if we are going to trust in God alone then we must make God our top priority in our lives. Oftentimes we say we love and worship God alone, but we don't give God first place in our lives. Whatever we prioritize most is what we truly worship. If we put our jobs or careers before God, then we worship our jobs or careers. If we put our families before God, then we worship our families. If we put things before God, then we worship things. Remember who or whatever we worship we must depend on it to provide for us. Matthew 6:33 says *Seek ye first the Kingdom of God and His righteousness and all these things shall be added unto you.* If we prioritize God first, then He will provide everything that we need.

Your day is already blessed!

DAY 19

As Christians if we are going to trust in God alone then we must realize that we must surrender ourselves totally and completely to God. One of the biggest problems that many Christians have is surrendering control of their lives to Christ. Many people who call themselves Christians want to have Jesus as their Savior, but they don't want to surrender to Christ as Lord. They want to be able to do what they want to do and say what they want to say and act how they want to act but still say that Jesus is their Lord and Savior. When Jesus is our Lord and Savior then we must surrender our will to His will. In Mark 8:35(NLT) Jesus says *If you try to hang onto your life, you will lose it. But if you give up your life for My sake and for the sake of the Good News, you will save it.* So, it's very simple surrender your life to Jesus's control and save your life or you maintain control of your life and lose it.

Your day is already blessed!

DAY 20

As Christians if we are going to trust in God alone then we must realize that God is our protection and our dwelling place in the times of trouble. The psalmist wrote that God is our refuge and strength a very present help in the time of trouble. In these trying times we must hold fast to that. When we see all the negative things happening in the world today, the disasters that are destroying people's lives and homes. What gives us hope is the Word of God. Psalms 119:114 says *You are my refuge and my shield; Your word is my source of hope.* Without knowing that this world is not my home life could be depressing but because I know who's in control and greater is coming. I give God praise.

> Your day is already blessed!

DAY 21

As Christians if we are going to trust in God alone then we must demonstrate God's love to one another. So many people who call themselves Christians say that they love God but the don't show that love to one another. If we love God, then we must obey God and love one another. 2 John 1:6(NLT) says Love means doing what God has commanded us, and He has commanded us to love one another, just as you heard from the beginning. Jesus says in John's gospel if you love Me keep My commandments and then He commands us to love one another as He has loved us. So, are we loving others the way Christ loves us?

Your day is already blessed!

DAY 22

As Christians if we are going to trust in God alone then we must do what God requires of us to do as His people. 2 Chronicles 7:14 says If My people, which are called by My name, will humble themselves, and pray, and seek My face, and turn from their wicked ways; then will I hear from heaven, and will forgive their sin and heal their land. We're so busy complaining about what the government ain't doing or what the folks in the world is doing that we've lost sight of what we as God's people still fail to do. God is waiting on His people to humble themselves instead of being so prideful and high-minded like they more than anybody else. He's waiting on us to pray about everything and not just talk about everything. God is waiting for us to seek His face to look to Him for guidance instead of watching the news or social media. God is waiting on us to turn from our wicked ways and stop shining the light on others public wickedness while we hide our private wickedness. If we want our world to change it starts with us.

You day is already blessed!

DAY 23

As Christians if we are going to trust in God alone then we be thankful that God refreshes our souls and leads in the right path. For Psalms 23:3(NLT) says *He refreshes my soul. He guides me along the right path for His name's sake.* When we are weary and worn, He refreshes our soul. When we are worried and fearful, He refreshes our souls. When we are angry and resentful, He refreshes our souls. Not only will He refresh our souls, but He also leads us along the right path. When we get off track, He leads us back to the right path and He does it for His name's sake. Because we go out bearing His name and He doesn't want us making His name bad. So, thank God for refreshing your soul and leading you along the right path.

Your day is already blessed!

DAY 24

As Christians if we are going to trust in God alone then we must trust His peace to rule in our lives. During these trying times there seems to be so much turmoil, trials and tribulations on every hand. People seem to be so stressed-out suffering from the anxiety of what might happen that we forget that God is still in control and He's the One calling the shots. Not the president not the governor not the mayor nor the economist God is in control. So, we need to do what Colossians 3:15 says *and let the peace of God rule in your hearts, to the which also ye are called in one body: and be ye thankful.* Let means to allow or permit or yield to. Peace is Sha Lomé which means wholeness nothing missing. Rule means to call the shots. So, we need to allow the wholeness of God's peace to call the shots in our lives and just be thankful.

Your day is already blessed!

DAY 25

As Christians if we are going to trust in God alone then we must continue to confess that Jesus Christ is Lord, and we can't just confess it with our mouths we must believe it in our hearts. You see many people who call themselves Christians say the words but the way that they behave doesn't line up with what they're saying. What we truly believe will determine how we behave. So, if we believe that Jesus has been given a name that is above every other name and that at the name of Jesus every knee will bow, and every tongue shall confess that Jesus is Lord to the glory of God then we will behave like we believe.

Your day is already blessed!

DAY 26

As Christians if we are going to trust in God alone then we must realize that God places people in our lives to help us to see Him more. A true friend that's a brother or sister in Christ is a valuable asset to have in this life. A true friend is someone that you can pour your heart out to and trust that they won't share it with others one that you can share your weaknesses and vulnerability with, and they won't judge you. One that is authentic and honest who will tell you the truth with love even when it hurts. Proverbs 17:17 says *A friend loveth at all times, and a brother is born for adversity.* If you have a friend or a brother or sister like that thank God for them. If you don't ask God for them.

Your day is already blessed!

DAY 27

As Christians if we are going to trust in God alone then we must continue to keep our minds on the things of God. Too many people who call themselves Christians are focused on the things of the world more than they are on the things of God. They're more concerned about what the news says or what's trending on social media or what's the latest gossip is than they are on what the Word of God says. We find ourselves suffering from worry, fear and anxiety because we're thinking about the wrong things. Philippians 4:8(NLT) says *and now dear brothers and sisters, one final thing. Fix your thoughts on what is true and honorable and right and pure and lovely and admirable.* Think about things that are excellent and worthy of praise. All of these describe God and His Word. So, think about that.

You day is already blessed!

DAY 28

As Christians if we are going to trust in God alone then we must not believe the lies of Satan we must believe the truth of God's Word. Satan always lies to God's people and one of his greatest lies is that you're not enough or you don't have enough. Simply put he wants us to think that we are not who God says we are. Satan was successful with this tactic with Adam and Eve, but he failed with Jesus because Jesus knew who He was, and He used the truth against Satan's lies. We can't believe Satan's lies we have to know that we are who God says we are and that with God we have and are more than enough. Jesus says in John 10:10 *The thief cometh, but for to steal and to kill, and to destroy I am come that they might have life and might have it more abundantly.* Enjoy your abundant life.

Your day is already blessed!

DAY 29

As Christians if we are going to trust in God alone then we must remember to thank God for His Spirit that dwells in us. We spend a lot of time thanking God for giving His only begotten Son to die on the cross for our sins and that good however we also need to thank God for sending us His Spirit to reveal Christ to us and to dwell in us. The Holy Spirit guides us from day to day. He guides us into all truths, and He produces love joy peace longsuffering gentleness goodness meekness faith and temperance in our lives. So, let's thank our Father for giving us His Spirit.

Your day is already blessed!

DAY 30

As Christians if we are going to trust in God alone then we must understand that trusting in God gives us perfect peace. Isaiah 26:3-4(NLT) says *You will keep in perfect peace* all who trust in You, all whose thoughts are fixed on You! Trust in the Lord always, for the Lord God is the eternal Rock. When we totally rely upon God in everything and for everything then we have no need to worry or fear and that's what perfect peace feels like. But we must always trust God because He is our everlastingly Rock and when we stand upon the Rock no storm in life can bring us down. Oh yeah, we may get hit by the waves but because the Rock is unmovable so are we.

Your day is already blessed!

DAY 31

As Christians if we are going to trust in God alone then we must stand strong and press forward in the face of adversity from our adversaries. Satan, the world and our flesh are all trying to get us to turn away from God and they are using many different tactics. But we must remember that no weapon that is formed against us shall prosper. It doesn't mean that weapons won't be formed it just means that it won't defeat us. Why? Because we have been given victory through our Lord and Savior Jesus Christ. 1 Corinthians 15:57-58 says Thanks be unto God, which giveth us the victory through our Lord Jesus Christ. Therefore, my beloved brethren, be ye steadfast, unmovable, always abounding in the work of the Lord, for as much as ye know that your labor is not in vain in the Lord.

Your day is already blessed!

DAY 32

As Christians if we are going to trust in God alone then we must learn how to give unto others. I know many people may say that they don't have anything to give during these trying times. Giving is not always about money. When Peter and John encountered the lame man at the gate, they said silver and gold have I none but such as I have, I give unto you in the name of Jesus rise up and walk and the man stood leaping and praising God. We serve a giving God. For God so loved the world that He gave. Paul quotes Jesus in Acts 20:35 *It is more blessed to give than it is to receive.* Don't make the mistake of believing that every resource that comes to you is for your consumption only. God blessed you to be a blessing.

Your day is already blessed!

DAY 33

As Christians if we are going to trust in God alone then we must rest in His peace. With so much turmoil in the world today with the pandemic and so many other trials and tribulations that we face we have a gift from our Lord and Savior Jesus Christ. Jesus says in John 14:27(NLT) I am leaving you with a gift—peace of mind and heart. And the peace I give is a gift that the world cannot give. So, don't be troubled or afraid. Too many people who call themselves Christians are seeking peace from the wrong source. Nothing of the world can give us peace. We need the peace from God which surpasses all understanding for that peace will keep our hearts and minds from being troubled and fearful.

Your day is already blessed!

DAY 34

As Christians if we are going to trust in God alone then we must look to God in every situation and circumstance in our lives. Too often we think we can handle situations on our own and we don't look to God for guidance, and we end up making the situation worse instead of better. Or we may say that I don't need to bother God with this little problem and again we try to handle it ourselves and a little problem becomes a big problem simply because we didn't seek God. 1 Chronicles 16:11 says *Seek the Lord and His strength, seek His face continually.* So, no matter how small something may seem or how big it maybe we should seek the Lord continually and let Him handle our situations.

Your day is already blessed!

DAY 35

As Christians if we are going to trust in God alone then we must trust God to show us the way. Lord show us the way to love in-spite of hateful racism and social injustice. Lord show us the way to endure the hardships of dealing with loss, hurt and disappointment. Lord show us the way to walk through the valley of the shadow of death and not be fearful. Psalms 16:11(NLT) says You will show me the way of life, granting me with Your presence and the pleasures of living with You forever. God has shown us the way it's looking unto Jesus the author and finisher of our faith.

Your day is already blessed!

DAY 36

As Christians if we are going to trust in God alone then we must continue to maintain a positive attitude in the midst of these trying times. I know that many of us have lost jobs, loved ones and friends during these trying times but what we cannot lose is our hope. As a matter of fact, Romans 12:12(NLT) says Rejoice in our confident hope. Be patient in trouble and keep on praying. No matter how bad it seems rejoice in our confident hope and be patient in trouble, because trouble don't last always. So just keep praying and God will see us through.

Your day is already blessed!

DAY 37

As Christians if we are going to trust in God alone then we must realize that we have all that we need to live a godly life. Oftentimes we find ourselves wanting more of this and more of that and we realize that when we get the more it still doesn't satisfy us. That's because our focus is too much on the things of the world than on living a godly life. But once we realize that living a godly life is really the good life and we understand that Jesus is all we need for that godly living then life is wonderfully blessed. 2 Peter 1:3(NLT) says By *His divine power*, God has given us everything we need for living a godly life. We have received all of this by coming to know Him, the One Who called us to Himself by means of His marvelous glory and excellence.

Your day is already blessed!

DAY 38

As Christians if we are going to trust in God alone then we must not put our focus so much on what's in front of us, but we need to focus on Who we trust and what He's promised. We spend so much time focusing on the cares of this world and all the negative things that are happening around us, but we fail to realize that all these things are temporary because this world is not our home. We are citizens of the Kingdom of God and God has prepared a beautiful home for us to dwell in for all eternity. So, our focus should be as Paul says in 2 Corinthians 4:17-18(NLT) *For our present troubles are small and won't last very long. Yet they produce for us a glory that vastly outweighs them and will last forever.* So, we don't look at the troubles we can see now; rather, we fix our gaze on things that cannot be seen. For the things we see now will soon be gone, but the things we cannot see will last forever.

       Your day is already blessed!

DAY 39

As Christians if we are going to trust in God alone then we must stay faithful to God during these trying times. I pray that in the midst of all these troubles, trials and tribulations that we are all trusting and believing that God will see us through, and that God will bless every endeavor that we seek to do in His name. For we constantly face racial injustice and systemic racism, but I pray as Paul prayed in 2 Thessalonians 1:11-12 *With this in mind, we constantly pray for you, that our God may make you worthy of His calling, and that by His power He may bring to fruition every desire for goodness and your every deed prompted by faith.* We pray this so that the name of our Lord Jesus May be glorified in you, and you in Him, according to the grace of our God and Lord Jesus Christ.

                                          Your day is already blessed!

DAY 40

As Christians if we are going to trust in God alone then we must be willing to open ourselves up for God to search our hearts. Many people who call themselves Christians are abusive with their criticism of others to try to make themselves look good. But if our hearts are not right before God then we must ask God to search our hearts. Psalms 139:23-24(NLT) says Search me, O God, and know my heart; test me and know my anxious thoughts. Point out anything in me that offends You and lead me along the path of everlasting life. When God searches our hearts then we can speak the truth in love without beating people up with the truth. We will build people up instead of tearing people down.
Your day is already blessed!

DAY 41

As Christians if we are going to trust in God alone then we must realize that God's Word is not just informative, but it is also transformative. Many people think that because they read the Bible and can quote some scriptures that they know enough but these people are usually just full of information, but they have received no revelation. Information says I can tell you what it says. Revelation says I can tell you what it means and apply it in my life. It's when we get revelation that we then see transformation which is a change in character or condition. Romans 12:2 says *and be not conformed to this world: but be ye transformed by the renewing of your mind, that you may prove what is that good, and acceptable, and perfect will of God.* So, is the Word just informative to you or is it transformative?

Your day is already blessed!

DAY 42

As Christians if we are going to trust in God alone then we must not be fearful. Satan tries to use so many things in this world to make us fearful, but we must understand that no matter what is going on around God still loves us and He will always take care of us and provide for us. Many people who call themselves Christians really don't know the love of God for themselves because they don't know God themselves. Oh, they know about Jesus because they have received a lot of information about who He is. But what they are missing is the revelation of who He is. When we have a personal relationship with Jesus, He reveals Himself to us in a way that we know Him intimately and that intimate relationship cast out all fears. Do you really know Jesus, or do you just know about Him?

Your day is already blessed!

DAY 43

As Christians if we are going to trust in God alone then we must learn not to return evil for evil. When someone does us wrong, we can't return wrong to them because all that does is create more wrong. There is a lot of evil in this world and the only way to overcome it is by doing good. Romans 12:21 says *Be not overcome of evil but overcome evil with good.* Dr. King taught us that we can't overcome hatred with hatred for only love can overcome hatred. So, allow God to deal with whoever or whatever has wronged you because when He handles it **ITS ALL GOOD.**

Your day is already blessed!

DAY 44

As Christians if we are going to trust in God alone then we must continue to confess our sins. Satan wants to use what we've done to make us feel guilty and condemned but we may be guilty but there is no condemnation for those who are in Christ Jesus. So, we must be open with God like David in Psalms 51:1-2 Have mercy on me O God according to Thy lovingkindness: according unto the multitude of Thy tender mercies blot out my transgressions. Wash me thoroughly from my iniquity, and cleanse me from my sin. So, don't let Satan and people condemn you confess and be cleansed by the blood of Jesus for we are covered by His blood; forgiven by His mercy; and loved by His grace.

Your day is already blessed!

DAY 45

As Christians if we are going to trust in God alone then we must learn how to love our enemies. It's human nature to want to return evil for evil to want to do something to someone who has wronged you. But we are not controlled by human nature because we are children of God and we have taken on His nature. Matthew 5:43-45a(NLT) Jesus says *You have heard the law that says, "Love your neighbor "and hate your enemies. But I say love your enemies!* Pray for those who persecute you! In that way you will be acting as true children of your Father in Heaven. Are you truly acting as a child of God?

Your day is already blessed!

DAY 46

As Christians if we are going to trust in God alone then we must have the right attitude to be joyful, the fortitude to be prayerful and gratitude to be thankful. No matter what is going on in our lives we must be joyful, because the more joyful we are in the Lord the stronger we become. Remember the Joy of the Lord is our strength. Fortitude is courage in pain or adversity. So, when we have the courage to pray in the midst of our pain and adversity then we have the fortitude to remain prayerful. We must have the gratitude, which is the quality of being thankful for when we are thankful in everything, we are fulfilling God's will. 1 Thessalonians 5:16-18(NLT) says *Always be joyful. Never stop praying. Be thankful in all circumstances, for this is God's will for you who belong to Christ Jesus.*

Your day is already blessed!

DAY 47

As Christians if we are going to trust in God alone then we must realize that we are ultimately God's servants. We do have to serve others as a servant of God and many of us get frustrated and want to quit serving because we're looking for appreciation and praise from the people, we serve rather than from the God we truly serve. We're more concerned about what people think or how people feel about us than we are about what God feels about us. Colossians 3:23-24(NLT) says *Work willingly at whatever you do, as though you were working for the Lord rather than for people.* Remember that the Lord will give you an inheritance as your reward, and that the Master that you are serving is Christ.

Your day is already blessed!

DAY 48

As Christians if we are going to trust in God alone then we must understand that what we go through is not for our detriment but it's for our betterment. Tests and trials come in our lives to help to build up our endurance. So, we must have the right attitude when troubles come James 1:2-4(NLT) says *Dear brothers and sisters, when troubles of any kind come your way, consider it an opportunity for great joy. For you know that when your faith is tested, your endurance has a chance to grow. So, let it grow, for when your endurance is fully developed, you will be perfect and complete, needing nothing.* Our faith must be tested for us to be complete mature Christians.

Your day is already blessed!

DAY 49

As Christians if we are going to trust in God alone then we must have reverential fear of the Lord. Reverential fear is to be at awe with honor and respect. This reverential fear of the Lord is the foundation for God's wisdom in our lives. Knowing the Holy One gives us understanding. Proverbs 9:10-12(NLT) says *Fear of the Lord is the foundation of wisdom.* Knowledge of the Holy One results in good judgment. Wisdom will multiply your days and add years to your life. If you become wise, you will be the one to benefit. If you scorn wisdom, you will be the one who suffers. So, if you want to multiply your days and add years to your life it all starts with a reverential fear for God.

Your day is already blessed!

DAY 50

As Christians if we are going to trust in God alone then we must have a heart for the things that God has a heart for. The reason God trusted David so much was because God said that David was a man after God's own heart. Even though David committed adultery and murder God still trusted David. But David knew he needed God to do something for him, so he asked God in Psalms 51:10 *Create in me a clean heart, O God; and renew a right spirit within me.* David knew that his heart had to be right for him to do God's will. We must download God's heart into our hearts if we want to do God's will. Remember Blessed are the pure in heart for they shall see God.

Your day is already blessed!

DAY 51

As Christians if we are going to trust in God alone then we must learn how to wait on God with expectancy knowing that His Word will come to pass. We must have expectation like a farmer. When a farmer plants a crop, he then begins to prepare for a harvest. Sometimes he has to remove the weeds that are trying to hinder the growth from around his plants. Sometimes if there's a drought, he may have to water his plants, but he does this expecting a harvest. Psalms 130:5(AMPC) *says I wait for the Lord, I expectantly wait, and in His Word do I hope.* What Word from the Lord are you expectantly waiting for and hoping in? What are you doing while you wait?

Your day is already blessed!

DAY 52

As Christians if we are going to trust in God alone then we must realize that we must depend upon God for strength. Too many people who call themselves Christians are trying to live an independent life. Trusting in their own strength and doing things the way that they want to do them. But the Christian life is a life of dependency we have to depend upon God for everything especially for strength. Ephesians 6:10 says *Finally, my brethren, be strong in the Lord and in the power of His might.* We don't have the strength on our own to be able to withstand all that this life will throw at us. That's why we must trust in the Lord. Isaiah 40:31(NLT) says *But those who trust in the Lord will find new strength. They will soar high on wings like eagles. They will run and not grow weary. They will walk and not faint.*

                                Your day is already blessed!

DAY 53

As Christians if we are going to trust in God alone then we must be the light of the world that God has called us to be. You see the reason the world seems so dark today is that the people who call themselves Christians are not letting their lights shine so the world can see that there is hope in the midst of these dark times. So called Christians are hiding their lights when they should be letting their lights shine. We let our light shine when we show others the love of God. It may be through our service to others. It may be an encouraging word in a dark hour. Whatever God gives you as a light do what Matthew 5:16 says *Let your light shine before men, that they may see your good works, and glorify your Father which is in heaven.*

Your day is already blessed!

DAY 54

As Christians if we are going to trust in God alone then we must trust that whatever God allows in our lives God will cause to work together for our good and for His glory. Romans 8:28 says *and we know that all things work together for good to them that love God, to them that are the called according to His purpose.* Now that doesn't mean that all things will feel good or seem good or look good, but God will work it for our good. Many people are saying it's so sad that all these people have lost their homes in the hurricane and that is sad but if they have good insurance, they will be living in a brand-new home. I know they'll be displaced for a while, but God will work it for their good and then they will give Him the glory. So, whatever you're going through right now know that it's working for your good and for His glory. And if it ain't good He ain't through working.

Your day is already blessed!

DAY 55

As Christians if we are going to trust in God alone then we must understand that God is faithful, and His love is everlasting, and His mercies are renewed daily. Lamentations 3:22-23 says *It is of the Lord's mercies that we are not consumed, because His compassions fail not. They are new every morning: great is Thy faithfulness.* God is not holding our past failures or our shortcomings or our current struggles against us if we confess them to Him. He has brand new mercy waiting for us today. And if God is not holding these things against us then why do we allow others or ourselves to hold them against us. Remember if we confess our sins God is faithful to forgive us and cleanse us from all unrighteousness.

Your day is already blessed!

DAY 56

As Christians if we are going to trust in God alone then we must realize and understand that God is always there for us. He understands that we sometimes grow weary, and we sometimes get discouraged. When we look at all the negative things that are happening in this world, we can become discouraged. When we look at how we struggle to keep our heads above water, and it seems like every time we take one step forward, we fall five steps back we can grow weary. But the good news is in Jeremiah 31:25(NLT) God says *For I have given rest to the weary and joy to the sorrowing*. And in Matthew 11:28-30 Jesus gives us an invitation Then Jesus said, Come to Me, all of you who are weary and carry heavy burdens, and I will give you rest. Take My yoke upon you. Let Me teach you, because I am humble and gentle at heart, and you will find rest for your souls. For My yoke is easy to bear, and the burden I give you is light. So, when you find yourself growing weary and discouraged just trust and lean on the Lord and He will give you rest and encouragement.

Your day is already blessed!

DAY 57

As Christians if we are going to trust in God alone then we can't grow weary in well doing. Oftentimes we find ourselves getting tired of doing what's right especially when it seems like we're not getting anywhere and those who aren't doing right seem to be prospering. But we can't allow what seems to be to override what the Word of God says. Galatians 6:9 says and let us not be weary in well doing: for in due season, we shall reap, if we faint not. I know that serving others and there seems like no reward can cause you to be sick and tired of doing it. But we have got to know that there is a harvest ready for us and we will reap that harvest if we don't quit if we stay steadfast unmovable always abounding in the work of the Lord knowing that our labor is not in vain. Be encouraged my brothers and sisters' due season is on the way.

Your day is already blessed!

DAY 58

As Christians if we are going to trust in God alone then we must continue to stand firm on the morals and standards of God's Word. No matter how people feel about it or whatever people may say about you and no matter how your situation may seem you must keep the faith and not allow fear and doubt to deter you from being who God called you to be. 1 Corinthians 16:13-14(NLT) says *Be on guard. Stand firm in the faith. Be courageous. Be strong. And do everything with love.* So, watch and stand courageously and strong and do it all in love for God and your fellow man.

Your day is already blessed!

DAY 59

As Christians if we are going to trust in God alone then we must continue to do the right thing. We must continue to love others and be merciful and gracious towards others even when they don't appreciate you for it or when they take your kindness for weakness. It can be very discouraging when you're doing what's right and people try to take advantage of you. They take advantage of your generosity. They take advantage of your loving kindness. But Galatians 6:9(NLT) says *So let's not get tired of doing what is good. At just the right time we will reap a harvest of blessing if we don't give up.* So be encouraged your harvest is on the way just keep doing good.

Your day is already blessed!

DAY 60

As Christians if we are going to trust in God alone then we must realize that even in the midst of what we are going through we must still rejoice with confident hope. No matter how bad your problems may seem now whether they are financial problems or relationship problems or physical problems we can rejoice because we know that God is going to use our situation to make us better. Romans 5:3-5(NLT) says *We can rejoice, too, when we run into problems and trials, for we know that they help us to develop endurance. And endurance develops strength of character, and character strengthens our confident hope of salvation. And this hope will not lead to disappointment. For we know how dearly God loves us, because He has given us the Holy Spirit to fill our hearts with His love.* So, whatever you're going through right now rejoice because God is making you better.

Your day is already blessed!

DAY 61

As Christians if we are going to trust in God alone then we must understand that there is only one way for men to be saved. That is through our Lord and Savior Jesus Christ, who gave His life as a ransom for our sins. 1 Timothy 2:5-6(NLT) says For, *there is one God and one mediator that can reconcile God and humanity—the man Christ Jesus. He gave His life to purchase freedom for everyone.* This is the message that God gave to the world at just the right time. Sin had separated man from God so God allowed Christ Jesus to come and take on flesh as a man so that He could pay the price for all of mankind's sin. When we believe that Jesus has paid the price for our sins then we are reconciled back to God.

Your day is already blessed!

DAY 62

As Christians if we are going to trust in God alone then we must realize that if we say that we are in Christ then it should show in the way that we live. Christian means to be Christlike so as a Christian we should be loving and compassionate and gracious. Many people who call themselves Christians have no love for others they only think of themselves and they have no compassion for the needs of others they are only concerned about their needs being met and they certainly aren't gracious towards others who may have wronged them and don't deserve their forgiveness. But that's not how Jesus lived. 1 John 2:6(NLT) says *Those who say they live in God should live their lives as Jesus did.* Are you living a life of love and compassion and grace towards others?

Your day is already blessed!

DAY 63

As Christians if we are going to trust in God alone then we must realize that we can't have fellowship with God and still walk in darkness. Many people who call themselves Christians are still walking in darkness. They think that they can get away with declaring Christ publicly but living a life of sin privately. But it doesn't work that way because God knows and sees all things. 1 John 1:6-7(NLT) says *So we are lying if we say that we have fellowship with God but go on living in spiritual darkness; we are not practicing the truth. But if we are living in the light, as God is in the light, then we have fellowship with each other and the blood of Jesus, His Son, cleanse us from all sin.* Living in the light exposes who we really are and that's when we can have true fellowship with one another. Are you living in the light?

Your day is already blessed!

DAY 64

As Christians if we are going to trust in God alone then we must realize that we must find joy in going through many trials and tribulations. We must understand that if we're going through a trial then that also implies that we are coming out this trial and since we know we're coming out then we should do what James 1:2-4(NIV) says *Consider it pure joy, my brothers and sisters, whenever you face trials of many kind, because you know that the testing of your faith produces perseverance. Let perseverance finish its work so that you may be mature and complete, not lacking anything.* We can't say we trust God if our faith has never been tested. A faith that can't be tested can't be trusted. If we truly trust God, then we know that He going to see us through whatever we are going through right now. SO, WE COUNT IT ALL JOY.

Your day is already blessed!

DAY 65

As Christians if we are going to trust in God alone then we must learn how to follow the Spirit in every area of our lives. Many people say that they are walking in the Spirit, but they only want to walk in what they want to walk in, and they only want to follow the Spirit when it's convenient for them. They say that they're walking in the Spirit, but they won't apologize when they are wrong, or they won't forgive others who have wronged them. Galatians 5:25(NLT) says *Since we are living by the Spirit, let us follow the Spirit's leading in every part of our lives.* We don't get to choose when we are going to follow the Spirit but say we're walking in the Spirit. If we're going to live by the Spirit of the Living God, then we must follow His Spirit at all times.

Your day is already blessed!

DAY 66

As Christians if we are going to trust in God alone then we must always remember that God is watching, and He is listening. I know sometimes with all the negative things happening in the world and the wicked seem to be prospering while the righteous seem to be suffering it seems like God is not watching what's going on and that He's not listening to the cry of His people. But we must trust and believe and know that God is truly watching and listening. 1 Peter 3:12 says *for the eyes of the Lord are over the righteous, and His ears are open to their prayers: but the face of the Lord is against them that do evil.* So, no matter how hard it seems God is watching and listening, and He will do what needs to be done.

Your day is already blessed!

DAY 67

As Christians if we are going to trust in God alone then we must not spend time worrying about tomorrow. So many people are so worried about the what-ifs of tomorrow that they can't enjoy the present of today. Matthew 6:34 says *Take therefore no thought for the morrow: for the morrow will take thought of the things of itself. Sufficient unto today are the evil thereof.* Jesus told Paul that His grace was sufficient enough for him and it's sufficient enough for us also. So why spend time and energy worrying about what might be when we know what is. Enjoy the grace and mercy of Christ Jesus today and don't worry because if we see tomorrow, we will see brand new mercy.

Your day is already blessed!

DAY 68

As Christians if we are going to trust in God alone then we must trust His peace to rule in our lives. During these trying times there seems to be so much turmoil, trials and tribulations on every hand. People seem to be so stressed-out suffering from the anxiety of what might happen that we forget that God is still in control and He's the One calling the shots. Not the president not the governor not the mayor nor the economist God is in control. So, we need to do what Colossians 3:15 says *and let the peace of God rule in your hearts, to the which also ye are called in one body: and be ye thankful.* Let means to allow or permit or yield to. Peace is Sha Lomé which means wholeness nothing missing. Rule means to call the shots. So, we need to allow the wholeness of God's peace to call the shots in our lives and just be thankful.

Your day is already blessed!

DAY 69

As Christians if we are going to trust in God alone then we must allow anything to cause us to think that God is not there for us. No matter what happens in our live we must know that God is always there to see us through. No matter how earth shaking or mountain moving the tragedies seem to be God has made us a promise. Isaiah 54:10(NLT) says *for the mountains may move and the hills disappear, but even then, My faithful love will remain.* My covenant of blessing will never be broken, says the Lord, who has mercy on you. So, it doesn't matter what you're going through right now don't let it shake your faith in God because He's always there to see you through.

Your day is already blessed!

DAY 70

As Christians if we are going to trust in God alone then we must focus on God's plan for our lives and not our own. We must trust that the plan that God has for us is better than anything that we can plan for ourselves. We must understand that no matter what we plan it is God who orders our steps. Proverbs 16:9(NLT) says We can make our plans, but the Lord determines our steps. So how do we know which way to go Hebrews 12:2a(NLT) says We do this by keeping our eyes on Jesus, the champion who initiates and perfects our faith. So, when we focus on Jesus, we will fulfill the plans that God has for us.

Your day is already blessed!

DAY 71

As Christians if we are going to trust in God alone then we must not allow our past to become a distraction. Many of us allow past hurts, or past failures or even past successes to become a distraction from what God has in our future. We can't move forward for looking back. Our focus should be forward not backward that's why when we're driving the windshield in front of us is much bigger than the mirror that shows what's behind us. Paul says it like this in Philippians 3:13-14 *Brethren, I count not myself to have apprehended: but this one thing I do, forgetting those things that are behind, and reaching forth unto those things which are before, I press towards the mark for the prize of the high calling of God in Christ Jesus.* Your enemies, the flesh, the world and Satan all want to remind you of your past and the way to overcome them is Submit yourself to God, resist the devil and he will flee from you.

Your day is already blessed!

DAY 72

As Christians if we are going to trust in God alone then we must stay focused on the task that God has given us to do. We can't allow the distractions of the world around us to cause us to lose focus on the work that God has given us to do. God has called us to be a witness to the world of His love and grace and mercy and that He has given His Son for us to be saved from our sin. We can't let what's happening with this pandemic or what the president is doing distract us. In Nehemiah 6:3 it says, *And I sent messengers to them, saying, I am doing a great work, so that I cannot come down: why should the work cease, whilst I come down to you.* We must be like Nehemiah and stay on the wall and stay focused on what God has given us to do.

Your day is already blessed!

DAY 73

As Christians if we are going to trust in God alone then we must guard our hearts. Proverbs 4:23(NLT) says *Guard your heart above all else, for it determines the course of your life.* We have to make sure that what's in our heart lines up with what God desires. For if we delight ourselves in God then God will give us the desires of our hearts. So, we have to guard our hearts from negativity, worldly influences, and fleshly desires because whatever is in our hearts will come out of us. So, let's fill our hearts with the love of God by hiding the Word of God in our hearts that our hearts may be pure for Blessed are the pure in heart for they shall see God.

Your day is already blessed!

DAY 74

As Christians if we are going to trust in God alone then we must trust that God is able. Many people want to see God do great and mighty things in their lives, but they don't want to have to do anything. They want to live any way they want be able to do whatever they want but God doesn't work that way. Ephesians 3:20 says *Now unto Him that is able to do exceedingly abundantly above all that we ask or think, according to the power that worketh in us.* You see God is able to do way more than anything we can think of to ask Him to do but He's only going to work according to the power that worketh is us. So, if we're not connected to the power source then even though God is able to do it. It won't work. In John 15:7 Jesus says *If ye abide Me and My Word abides in you then you can ask what you will, and it shall be done for you.* So, the power that worketh in us is the Word of God. Is the Word of God at work in you?

Your day is already blessed!

DAY 75

As Christians if we are going to trust in God alone then we must totally trust in God in such a time as this. The enemy wants to isolate us to try to steal, kill and destroy God's children. He wants to fill our heads with lies and try to get us to either feel hopeless or to have hope in the wrong people, places or things. That's why we must put our trust totally in God alone. Proverbs 3:5-6(NLT) says *Trust in the Lord with all your heart; do not depend on your own understanding. Seek His will in ALL THAT YOU DO, and He will show you which path to take.* Don't be deceived TRUST GOD.

Your day is already blessed!

DAY 76

As Christians if we are going to trust in God alone then we must stay away from evil. Evil desires and evil influences can cause us to get off track and miss the blessings that God has for us. David tells us how to be blessed in Psalms 1:1-2 Blessed is the man that walketh not in the counsel of the ungodly, nor standeth in the way of sinners, nor sitteth in the seat of the scornful. But his delight is in the law of the Lord; and in His law doth he meditate day and night. We can't let evil influences direct our decisions. Our decisions should be influenced by the Word of God. Solomon, who was the wisest man, tells his son in Proverbs 1:10 My son, if sinners entice thee, consent thou not. We have to realize that in times such as these people will offer you the world and make it seem enticing, but the choice is yours as to what to do.

Your day is already blessed!

DAY 77

As Christians if we are going to trust in God alone then we must be willing to do what God is calling us to do in such a time as these. The only way for us to know what we should be doing is to ask God for wisdom for James 1:5 says that if *we lack wisdom then we should ask God for wisdom and He gives it to us freely.* We need wisdom because Ecclesiastes 3:1-9 tells us there is a season and a purpose for everything like a time to plant and a time to pluck up what's planted, a time to laugh and a time to cry, a time to break down and a time to build up, a time to speak and a time to keep silent but only the wisdom of God can reveal to us what to do in such a time as this.

Your day is already blessed!

DAY 78

As Christians if we are going to trust in God alone then we must realize that we are called for such a time as this. In the book of Esther there was a decree signed by the king to destroy all the Jews not knowing that Esther the Queen was a Jew also. Esther's uncle sent her a message and Esther 4:14 says *for if thy altogether holdeth thy peace at this time, then shall there enlargement and deliverance arise to the Jews from a different place; but thou and thou father's house shall be destroyed: and who knoweth whether thou art come to the kingdom for such a time as this.* Just like Esther God has equipped and empowered us for such a time as this. He has given us talents, gifts and abilities to Glorify Him for such a time as this. We are called to go through what we're going through for such a time as this. So, are you glorifying God or complaining in such a time as this?

Your day is already blessed!

DAY 79

As Christians if we are going to trust in God alone then we must live out the complete will of God not just the part that we feel comfortable with. Sometimes living out God's will can hurt us now to help us later. Like maybe God wants us to let go of someone we think that we can't live without but they are not good for us and God is trying to get us where He wants us to be but we refuse to let go because it will hurt so much but it's better to hurt now in the will of God and let Him heal the hurt and bring you to where He wants you to be than to refuse and be outside the will of God. So, I pray for you as Epaphras prayed for the believers in Colossians 4:12 *that ye may stand perfect and complete in all the will of God.*

Your day is already blessed!

DAY 80

As Christians if we are going to trust in God alone then we must learn how to talk to others. Many people who call themselves Christians don't know how to talk to people. Their words are so abrasive and hurtful that people tune them out when they start talking or try to avoid them altogether. Paul tells believers how we ought to speak to others in Colossians 4:6 *Let your speech be always with grace, seasoned with salt, that ye may know how ye ought to answer every man.* We should speak with God's unmerited favor to others, and have it seasoned with salt because salt does several things 1 Salt melts coldness if you pour salt on ice it melts 2. Salt preserved before everyone had freezers, they used to salt the meat down to keep it fresh 3 Salt helps to heal wounds old people used to pour a little salt in an open wound to help it heal. Now it burned like the devil, but it helps it to heal. So, let's learn how to talk to others graciously and seasoned with salt.

Your day is already blessed!

DAY 81

As Christians if we are going to trust in God alone then we must learn how to live our lives wisely especially in the presence of unbelievers. For if we are going to be able to win others to Christ it's not going to be because of our knowledge of the Bible because if we just share our knowledge with them then they will only receive information but when we share the wisdom that comes from God then they get revelation because God speaks to them through the words of wisdom that He shared with us. We must make sure that we are prepared and ready to make the most of every opportunity that we are given to share Christ with others. That's why Paul told the believers in Colossians 4:5(NLT) Live wisely among those that are not believers and make the most of every opportunity. So, as you go throughout your day be ready to share the wisdom of Christ with anyone you come in contact with it may be just the Word that they need.

Your day is already blessed!

DAY 82

As Christians if we are going to trust in God alone then we must devote ourselves to prayer. If we want to see our land healed, then we must do what God told Solomon that If My people who are called by My name will humble themselves and pray and seek My face and turn from their wicked ways then will I hear from heaven and forgive their sins and heal their land. God is looking for prayer warriors during these trying times, so I instruct you as Paul instructed the believers in Colossians 4:2-4(NLT) Devote yourselves to prayer with an alert mind and a thankful heart. Pray for us, too, that God will give us many opportunities to speak about His mysterious plan concerning Christ. Pray that I will proclaim this message as clearly as I should.

Your day is already blessed!

DAY 83

As Christians if we are going to trust in God alone then we should be living our lives looking for the return of our Lord and Savior Jesus Christ. Too many people who call themselves Christians are not living their lives like Christ is soon to return. They act as if they have plenty of time, but we know not the day nor the hour when the Son of Man shall return but we have to be looking forward to His return. With all the fulfillments of prophecy we see these days we better be ready every day because judgement day is soon to come and those who think they are above judgement are going to have to bow down and confess that Jesus Christ is Lord.

Your day is already blessed!

DAY 84

As Christians if we are going to trust in God alone then we must understand that we must receive the Word of God with joy and that when we receive the Word with joy the Holy Spirit helps us to become more like Christ and when we become more like Christ, we become examples to the world of Who Christ is. The problem comes when people who call themselves Christians are not receiving the Word with joy and haven't had the Holy Spirit to make them more like Christ are becoming an example to the world and the world is labeling all Christians to be like the bad examples. That's why Paul encouraged the believers in 1 Thessalonians 1:6-7 *And you became followers of us, and of the Lord, having received the Word in much affliction, with joy of the Holy Ghost: So that ye were examples to all that believe in Macedonia and Achaia.* So, I encourage you to continue to receive the Word with joy and let the Holy Spirit continue to make you more like Christ so you can be an example of Christ to the world.

Your day is already blessed!

DAY 85

As Christians if we are going to trust in God alone then we must realize that we have been chosen by God to be His people. We are called of God to spread the Good News of Jesus Christ to this lost and dying world and we are failing as people of God because we are either not sharing the gospel or we are trying to share the gospel in our own power, but we must share the gospel with the power of the Holy Spirit. 1 Thessalonians 1:4-5(NLT) says *We know, dear brothers and sisters, that God loves you and has chosen you to be His own people. For when we brought you the Good News, it was not only with words but also with power, for the Holy Spirit gave you full assurance that what we said was true.* So, as we share the gospel let's pray that the Holy Spirit will not only give us the words to say but will also give assurance to the listeners that the Word is true.

Your day is already blessed!

DAY 86

As Christians if we are going to trust in God alone then we must continue to pray for one another. During these trying times Satan is busy trying to steal, kill and destroy as many of God's people as he can. During this time of isolation and people not assembling themselves in the House of the Lord Satan is trying to use his worldly devices to take our focus off of God. But I'm praying for you as Paul prayed for the believers in 1 Thessalonians 1:2-3(NLT) We always thank God for all of you and pray for you constantly. As we pray to our God and Father about you, we think of your faithful work, your loving deed, and the enduring hope you have because of our Lord Jesus Christ. I truly pray that you just remain faithful to God during these trying times. Trust Him and He will see you through.

Your day is already blessed!

DAY 87

As Christians if we are going to trust in God alone then we must understand that as the elect of God that we are chosen by Him to be holy and we have to be properly dressed for service. Colossians 3:12-14 says *Put on therefore, as the elect of God, holy and beloved, bowels of mercies, kindness, humbleness of mind, meekness, longsuffering; Forbearing one another, and forgiving one another, if any man have a quarrel against any: even as Christ forgave you, so also do ye. And above all these things put on charity, which is the bond of perfectness.* As God's chosen servant are you dressed for service?

Your day is already blessed!

DAY 88

As Christians if we are going to trust in God alone then we must realize that there are also some things that we must take off if we're going to live eternally with Christ. Colossians 3:8-9 says *but now ye also put off all these; anger, wrath, malice, blasphemy, filthy communication out of your mouth. Lie not one to another, seeing that you have put off the old man with his deeds. So, we can't live eternally with Christ if we're still holding on to anger, let it go before it grows into wrath then wrath festers into malicious acts.* We also must watch our mouths. Let not filthy words come out of our mouths and stop lying to one another about one another or on one another.

Your day is already blessed!

DAY 89

As Christians if we are going to trust in God alone then we must realize that we are to be dead to sin and walking in the newness of life. So, we must put some things to death. Colossians 3:5-7(NLT) says *So put to death the sinful, earthly things lurking within you. Have nothing to do with sexual immorality, impurity, lust and evil desires. Don't be greedy, for a greedy person is an idolater, worshipping the things of this world. Because of these sins the anger of God is coming. You used to do these things when your life was still a part of this world.* Oftentimes we are waiting on God to take things away from us when God is waiting for us to put it to death not just put it off but put it to death. Have your sinful worldly desires been put to death?

                      Your day is already blessed!

DAY 90

As Christians if we are going to trust in God alone then we must focus on the things of God. Oftentimes we spend too much time focusing on the things of this world and we forget that this world is not our home. We should focus our attention on heavenly things. Colossians 3:1-2 says *If ye then be risen with Christ, seek those things which are above, where Christ sitteth on the right hand of God. Set your affections on things above, not on things on the earth.* Jesus doesn't want us worrying about earthly things that's why He told us to Seek ye first the Kingdom of Heaven and all these things shall be added unto you. So, if you've been off track reprogram your spiritual GPS on heaven and let God take the wheel while you just enjoy the ride.

Your day is already blessed!

DAY 91

As that He will shield and protect us from the dangers of this life. With so many acts of senseless violence going on in the world today we have to take courage in knowing that God is our protector. If fact we should rejoice and shout for joy. Psalms 5:11-12 says but let all those that put their trust in Thee rejoice: let them ever shout for joy, because Thou defendeth them: let them also that love Thy name be joyful in Thee. For Thou, Lord, will bless the righteous; with favor wilt Thou compass him as with a shield. So not only will God protect us, but He also surrounds us with His favor. So, saints of God we should be shouting and rejoicing for God's protection and favor surrounds us daily.

Your day is already blessed!

DAY 92

As Christians if we are going to trust in God alone then we should know what God requires of us. Micah 6:8 says He hath shewed thee, o man, what is good; and what doth the Lord require of thee, but to do justly, and to love mercy, and to walk humbly with thy God? Jesus is our example of what's good. He lived His life doing justly or doing what was right. We should live our lives doing what's right. Not what we think or what we feel but what the Word of God says is right. We must love mercy. Jesus was merciful even on the cross when He said Father forgive them for, they know not what they do. It's easy for us to accept mercy towards us but we have to love to show mercy to others also. Though Jesus was God in the flesh He humbled Himself and walked humbly with God. We can't be high minded and prideful and say we're walking with God for God resists the proud, but He gives more grace to the humble. So, are you doing what God requires?

Your day is already blessed!

DAY 93

As Christians if we are going to trust in God alone then we must have a Christ-like attitude. Christian means to be Christlike so we need the mind of Christ to be Christlike. That means that we should do what Philippians 2:3-5 says Let nothing be done through strife or vainglory; but in lowliness of mind let each esteem other better than themselves. Look not every man on his own things, but every man also on the things of others. Let this mind be in you which was also in Christ Jesus. A Christlike attitude won't do anything for selfish ambition or glory for oneself. A Christlike attitude will think more of other and forget about himself/herself. For if you forget about self then when people wrong us then we won't quit because it's not about us. Do you have a Christlike attitude?

Your day is already blessed!

DAY 94

As Christians if we are going to trust in God alone then we are to walk together in unity. Jesus prays in John 17:21-23 that we would be one with one another as He and the Father are one. The Father in Christ and Christ in us through the Holy Spirit. For us to have unity with one another we must first get unified within ourselves. That means that we surrender to the leadership of the Holy Spirit in our lives. We give Him total authority over body soul and spirit. Then when we become unified within ourselves then we can unite with others who have been unified within themselves. Then we can walk as Paul said in Ephesians 4:3-6 Endeavoring to keep the unity of the Spirit in the bonds of peace. There is one body, and one Spirit, even as ye are called in one hope of your calling. One Lord, one faith, one baptism, One God and Father of all, who is above all, and through all and in you all. Let's walk in unity.

Your day is already blessed!

DAY 95

As Christians if we are not going to trust in God alone then we have to learn how to patiently wait on the Lord. But know that you're not the only one waiting. There are many others in the waiting room also. It's like being at the doctor's office doesn't the wait seem shorter if you find a good book to read or if you engage in a good conversation and then the next thing you know they're calling you back to see the doctor. Well in God's waiting room the best book to pick up is the Bible because it encourages you that the One, you're waiting on is able to do what you need Him to do. The best conversation is in the fellowship of the saints of God who will be a witness of what He has done for them. Then we can do what Psalms 27:14 says Wait on the Lord: Be of good courage, and He shall strengthen thy heart: wait, I say, on the Lord. No matter what it is you're waiting for He Is Able to deliver.

Your day is already blessed!

DAY 96

As Christians if we are going to trust in God alone then we need to seek God through His Word. Many people think that they are seeking God because they go to church on Sunday and hear a Word or because they listen to praise music during the week. These are good things to do but to seek God requires more than that. We have to get into the Word of God on a daily basis ourselves and let God speak to us through His Word. When we seek God daily through the Word God will reveal to us our place in the Kingdom of God. While we're seeking the best job or car or house or more money, we need to be seeking God. Matthew 6:33 says Seek ye first the Kingdom of God and His righteousness and all these things shall be added unto you. Are you seeking God daily through His Word?

Your day is already blessed!

DAY 97

As Christians if we are going to trust in God alone then we should speak what God's Word says about us. As we seek God through His Word then we begin to speak the Word of God over our lives. Instead of speaking all the negative thoughts of the world that we live in and the people around us we just speak the Word only. Proverbs 18:21 says Death and life are in the power of the tongue: and they that love it shall eat the fruit thereof. So, when we speak the Word of God then we speak life, and we eat the fruit of the life that God has planned for us. But when we speak negative words then we must eat what those negative words produce. That's why I ask God to do what David asked in Psalms 141:3 Set a watch, O Lord, before my mouth; keep the door of my lips. I only want to speak God's Word into my life, and I feed on the Word of God.

Your day is already blessed!

DAY 98

As Christians if we are going to trust in God alone then we must have a personal relationship with Christ. Many people are satisfied with just having knowledge about Christ. They know what their mama says or what Big Mama says or what the pastor says or even what the songwriter says about Jesus but that's not enough because just because you know about someone doesn't mean you know them. You have to develop a personal relationship with them to really get to know them. We should want to know Christ like the Apostle Paul declares in Philippians 3:10a(AMP) [For my determined purpose is] that I may know Him [that I may progressively become more deeply and intimately acquainted with Him, perceiving and recognizing and understanding the wonders of His person more strongly and more clearly], this is how we should want to know Jesus. Do you know Him intimately?

Your day is already blessed!

DAY 99

As Christians if we are going to trust in God alone then we must learn to be content with where God has us. Many of us don't know how to be content with what God has blessed us with because we haven't been taught contentment. To be content means to be in a state of peaceful joy. We can have contentment whether we have a little or whether we have a lot. Many people lose what they have because they are not content with what they have so they are trying to get more and end up with less. I'm like the Apostle Paul in Philippians 4:11-13 Not that I speak in respect of want for I have learned, that in whatsoever state I am, therewith to be content. I know both how to be abased and I know how to abound: everywhere and in all things, I am instructed both to be full and to be hungry, both to abound and suffer need. I can do all things through Christ which strengthened me. Have you learned to be content?

Your day is already blessed!

DAY 100

As Christians if we are going to trust in God alone then we are going to have to keep our eyes on the prize. We can't keep looking at the past if we want what God has for us. Many of us spend too much time looking back and making excuses for why we haven't succeeded in life from who did us wrong to who held us back to who didn't give us what we needed. Just let it go we can't move forward in life looking backwards. We must take the attitude of the Apostle Paul in Philippians 3:13-14 Brethren, I count not myself to have apprehended: but this one thing I do, forgetting those things that are behind, and reaching forth to those things which are before, I press towards the mark of the prize of the high calling of God in Christ Jesus. I'm living my life from the future back, focusing on spending eternity with Christ Jesus our Lord. Where's your focus?

Your day is already blessed!

DAY 101

As Christians if we are going to trust in God alone then speak with a spiritual boldness in Christ. Many of us are too timid when it comes to speaking about the things of Christ. Some of that is because of lack of knowledge. We don't speak because we don't know. People are looking for answers and the body of Christ should be pointing them to Jesus. Because whatever problems people may face Jesus is the answer. We have been given the boldness and confidence to let them know. Paul says in Ephesians 3:12 that we have a boldness in Christ and access with confidence by faith in Christ. Are you confident to speak the Word with boldness?

Your day is already blessed!

DAY 102

As Christians if we are going to trust in God alone then we must know that God will allow us to go through some hurtful situations in our lives. There will be times when we are broken hearted but Psalms 34:18 says that God draws closer to the broken-hearted. There are times when we will have to endure grief and sorrow and we will need God to comfort us but 2 Corinthians 1:3-4 says Blessed Be God, even the Father of our Lord Jesus Christ, the Father of mercies, and the God of all comfort, Who comforted us in all our tribulation, that we may be able to comfort them which are in any trouble, by the comfort wherewith we ourselves are comforted of God. So, God will allow us to go through pain that we may witness to others of how God comforted us in our time of pain. So, whatever you're going through know that God will comfort you and see you through.

Your day is already blessed!

DAY 103

As Christians if we are going to trust in God alone then we must walk in the Word of God. If we say that we have received Christ Jesus as our personal Lord and Savior, then we should walk(live) in Him. Colossians 2:6-7 says as ye have therefore received Christ Jesus the Lord, so walk ye in Him. Rooted and built up in Him, stablished in the faith, as ye have been taught, abounding therein with thanksgiving. So, we should walk in Christ, but it shouldn't just be a surface relationship we should be deeply rooted in Him. For the roots are what nourish the plant and the deeper the roots the stronger the plant will be. Then we must be built up in Christ and established in the faith. When our roots go down deep, we can be elevated high and being established in the faith we won't waver so that's something to be thankful for.

Your day is already blessed!

DAY 104

As Christians if we are going to trust in God alone then we must know the benefits of obeying His Word. Jesus says in John 15:14-15 Ye are My friends, if ye do whatsoever I command you. Henceforth I call ye not servants; do the servant knoweth not what his lord doeth: but I have called you friend; for all things that I have heard of My Father I have made known unto you. So, we become friends with Christ by obeying Him and when we obey Him, He reveals to us all the things that His Father has made known unto Him. So obeying Christ releases all the mysteries of the Kingdom of God. Jesus says in John 16:13-15 that the Holy Spirit will guide us into all truth and all things that the Father has belongs to Christ and the Spirit will show us all things. So, if we obey Christ, we get all things revealed to us.

Your day is already blessed!

DAY 105

As Christians if we are going to trust in God alone then we have to know that trusting Him gives us the ability to ask for what we want. Too many times we are afraid to ask God for what we want because we are afraid that our lives are not right, or we don't know if we should ask or not or maybe we don't know how God could bless us with something like that. But think back to when you were a child when you wanted something from your parents you didn't know how they were going to be able to provide what you wanted you just asked anyway. It was up to them how they were going to provide it. Matthew 7:7 says Ask, and it shall be given you; Seek, and ye shall find; knock, and it shall be open unto you. We don't have to worry about how God is going to provide it it's just our job to ask. What are you missing out on because you haven't asked?

                    Your day is already blessed!

DAY 106

As Christians if we are going to trust in God alone then we must be willing to be used by Him to draw others to Christ. Jesus wants to use us like He used the waterpots in His first miracle at the wedding in Cana recorded in John 2:1-11. Jesus was invited to a wedding and His mother came to Him and told Him they were out of wine. Jesus first rebuked His mother and said it was not His time, but she told the servants whatever He tells you to do you do it. Jesus told the servants to fill 6 big waterpots with water and then take them to the head of the feast and ladle it out to him. When the servants did what Jesus told them to do the water was turned into wine. Just like the waterpots Jesus wants to fill us with the water of the Holy Spirit and then He wants us to go out into the world and ladle out that water to others and as we ladle out the water of the Spirit to others, He changes it to the wine of joy. Are you willing to be a waterpot?

Your day is already blessed!

DAY 107

As Christians if we are going to trust in God alone then we must seek to sow fruits of righteousness. James 3:18 says and the fruit of righteousness is sown in peace of them that make peace. So, if we are going to sow the fruit of righteousness in the world then we need to be peacemakers and not hell raisers. Jesus says in Matthew 5:9 Blessed are the peacemakers: for they shall be called the children of God. We say that we are God's children so we should be peacemakers. Romans 12:18 says If it be possible, as much as lieth in you, live peaceably with all men. We have to seek peace and pursue peace according to 1 Peter 3:11. So are you sowing the fruit of righteousness?

Your day is already blessed!

DAY 108

As Christians if we are going to trust in God alone then we must not focus on our problems but focus on our problem solver. God is there for us to solve any problem that we may encounter. We just have to learn to take everything to God in prayer. The songwriter wrote What a friend we have in Jesus all our sins and griefs to bare what a privilege to carry everything to God in prayer. Philippians 4:6-7 says Be careful for nothing; but in everything by prayer and supplication with thanksgiving let your requests be made known unto God. And the peace of God, which surpasses understanding, shall keep your hearts and minds through Christ Jesus. So, if we take all our problems to the problem solver then He will give us peace. Where is your focus?

Your day is already blessed!

DAY 109

As Christians if we are going to trust in God alone then we must learn to let go of the past and stop letting it hinder the new thing that God wants to do in our lives. Too many people let things that happen in their past keep them looking backwards and they can't progress into the future that God has for them because they're stumbling over things looking backwards. If someone has hurt, you in the past forgive them and move on not for their sake but for yours. If there's something wrong that you regret doing, ask God to forgive you and forgive yourself and move. God wants to do a new thing in your life. Isaiah 43:18-19 says Remember ye not the former things, neither consider the things of old. Behold, I will do a new thing; it shall spring forth; shall ye not know it? I will even make a way in the wilderness, and rivers in the desert. So, look forward to God making a way out of no way and bringing living water into the dry places in your life. Let God do a new thing in your life.

Your day is already blessed!

DAY 110

As Christians if we are going to trust in God alone then we must do His works and His will without complaining and arguing amongst ourselves. Oftentimes the world is looking at us as Christians and they see us complaining and arguing amongst ourselves and they think why I should be a part of that. They don't see any difference between the church and the world. If we are going to draw the world to Christ, we have to be lights in the world. Philippians 2:14-15 says Do all things without murmuring and disputing: That ye may be blameless and harmless, the sons of God, without rebuke, in the midst of a crooked and perverse nation, among whom ye shine as lights in the world. So, let us stop complaining and arguing amongst ourselves and be lights of God unto the world.

Your day is already blessed!

Rev. Quincy K. Patterson was born August 9, 1966 to Mr. Tommy Patterson Sr and Mrs. Mary Alice Patterson in Starkville, MS. He is the youngest of seven siblings. Two brothers Willie Hinton and Tommy Patterson Jr and four sisters Rilla Simmons, Mary Patterson-Davis, Kathy Jean Davis and Cathy Jane Brown. Rev. Patterson is a 1984 graduate of Starkville High School where he was a member of championship football teams and a captain his senior year. Pastor Patterson then attended Mississippi Valley State University in Itta Bena, MS where he was a two-time Academic All-SWAC performer in football. During Rev. Patterson's senior year, he was elected the President of the Student Government Association. On May 7,

1988 He graduated with a Bachelor of Science Degree in Computer Science and Mathematics. He returned to Valley in 1990-1991 to complete his Mathematical Education certification. In August 1991 Rev. Patterson was able to fulfill one of his childhood dreams of returning to teach Mathematics in the Starkville School District teaching 3 years at Starkville High School and he spent 17 years directing misguided, misunderstood, and misbehaving students at Quad Alternative School. He retired in May 2011. Rev. Patterson accepted his call to the Gospel ministry in September of 1998 at the Springhill M. B. Church in Starkville, MS under Pastor Simeon T. Weatherby. He was elected the pastor of the Gospel Temple M. B. Church on May 7, 2000 and continues to serve in that capacity. On June 22, 2002 Rev. Patterson married the lovely Ms Natalie Hughes. Pastor Patterson's passion is preaching and teaching the Word of God with clarity and understanding. His motto is Building the Kingdom through Preaching, Teaching & Reaching